GiFTED AND TALENTED:
iQ TRaining

BRAINSTORM SERIES #4
Gifted and Talented Training
For Ages 3-6

2014 Edition

by **Pi For Kids Inc.**

4Kids
Learn To Innovate

Dr. Alex Pang

Stephanie Pang

Priscilla Wong

Raymond Pang

Owen Pang

Frankie Wong

Pi For Kids Inc.
Queens, New York,
USA
pi4kids.inc@gmail.com

Brainstorm: IQ Training
Gifted and Talented Training for Ages 3-6

Written and Published by: Pi For Kids Inc.

All of the questions in this book were written by:

Dr. Alex Pang   Priscilla Wong
Stephanie Pang   Raymond Pang
Owen Pang   Frankie Wong

ISBN-13: 978-1500720445
ISBN-10: 1500720445

Pi For Kids Inc.
Queens, New York,
USA
pi4kids.inc@gmail.com

The Theory of Multiple Intelligences

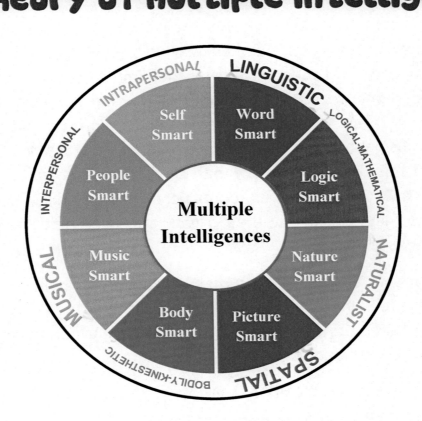

The Theory of Multiple Intelligences was developed by Howard Gardner, a psychologist and professor at Harvard, in 1983. He defines "intelligence" as the general ability to solve problems and learn new ideas. His theory includes 8 different types of intelligences that people use to interact with the world. Each person may use a mix these learning styles, but is usually prone to favor one specific one. For example, two children could both be strong in language, but one may be better in writing while the other is better at speaking. As a parent, we need to have confidence in our children's special abilities and support them as they travel their own path.

PI FOR KIDS, INC.

A note to parents and teachers:

One of the most important responsibilities or a parent or any child caregiver is to assess and acknowledge your child's strengths and potential. For a child to learn at their maximum level, we need to encourage their interests and allow them to find enjoyment in learning and exploring their talents. The definition of a gifted and talented child isn't just about the IQ measurement of "intelligence." Your child's gifted and talented abilities can be shown in various fields, such as art, music, math, writing, etc. Our job as parents is to accompany our children as they search for their strong suits and help them to pursue these interests.

According to scientific studies, usually children may show strengths in any one (or more) of the following categories. You may find it helpful to use this list when determining which your child is best at and which may need some more improvement:

1. **Memory:** Able to remember most of what they learn or hear
2. **Language Skills:** Able to remember and apply new vocabulary
3. **Wide Range of Interests**: Likes to try many different activities
4. **Thinking Abilities:** Able to think very fast on their feet
5. **Insight:** Able to read people and situations
6. **Justice and Perfection**: Likes to play fair and to keep things neat
7. **High Standards:** Has high expectations for themselves and others
8. **Sensitivity:** Able to take criticism and improve upon it
9. **Compassionate:** Has a big heart for people and certain situations
10. **Leadership:** Leads others, constructs plans and takes action

We wish you the best in this great journey to bring out your child's potential and to incite a joy for learning!

Sincerely,
Dr. Alex Pang
Pi FOR KiDS, inc.

Dear Parents,

One of the secrets to raising an intelligent learner is to emphasize the importance of education at a very young age. Though some children may be born with a uniquely high IQ, others may have to reach their potential by being given appropriate stimuli and training. The obstacle that many parents encounter in this process is finding the right resources.

We believe that "intelligence" does not only involve your IQ score. Rather, it is the combination of various skill sets and the ability to apply these skills to solve real-life problems. Our goal at PiForKids for publishing the Brainstorm series is to hone specific skill sets at a time and to provide the necessary tools for parents to encourage their children's growth.

Different parts of the brain control different functions. For instance, according to scientific studies, the left brain is mainly responsible for analytical and logical thinking, whereas the right brain controls our artistic, imaginative and language abilities.

The books, IQ Training and EQ Training of the BrainStorm series, are designed to evaluate and improve children's mental abilities. IQ, or the intelligence quotient, is a measurement of the way a child processes information. EQ, or the emotional quotient, is a indicator of how well a child manages his/her emotions. Both are critical for everyday life and future successes.

When using these workbooks, we suggest that teachers or parents read aloud the questions and encourage the child to explain his or her reasoning for each answer. Teachers and parents should also lead the child to think beyond the question and to consider how the answers would change accordingly if the questions were altered slightly.

Before the age of 5, children are most susceptible to learning because their brains are growing and developing rapidly. Early educational experiences are vital to every child's life, and we at Pi For Kids Inc. aspire to play a role in this journey that all children must take.

Sincerely,

Priscilla Wong &
Stephanie Pang
Pi FOR KiDS, iNC.

TABLE OF CONTENTS

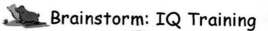

CRITICAL THINKING

Today is the little elephant's 4th birthday! He is very happy to celebrate with his friends. Can you use a red crayon to draw the right number of candles on the cake?

Pi For Kids Inc

 LANGUAGE

Oh no! A little dog cannot get out from the hole that it fell into! The little pig wants to help him, but doesn't know how. Using the objects shown in the picture, tell a story how the pig should help the dog.

LOGICAL THINKING

Do you know which animal has the longest neck? The longest tail? Use a red crayon to circle the longest neck animal, and use a blue crayon to circle the longest tail animal.

Pi For Kids Inc

OBSERVATION

What do you need when you go skiing? Use a blue crayon to circle the right objects below.

The pictures below tell a story about a family moving into a new house but the pictures are not in the right order! Use a pencil ✏ and write the numbers 1, 2, 3 or 4 in the white squares below to tell the order that the pictures should go.

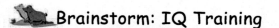

CRITICAL THINKING

What do you need when you go swimming? Use a green crayon to circle the right objects below.

OBSERVATION

What animals do you see on a farm? Use a purple crayon to circle the right animals below.

COUNTING

This little girl is helping her mother bake cookies. How many eggs are there in the carton? Use a pencil to write the number of eggs inside the circle.

 MATHEMATICS

There are 6 cookies in the tray, but there are 3 children! If each child gets the same number of cookies, how many will each of them get? Use a pencil ✏ to write the number in the circle below.

Pi For Kids Inc

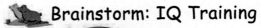

OBSERVATION

In this picture, there is only one animal without legs. Which animal is it? Use a blue crayon 🖍 to circle this animal.

MATHEMATICS

The cow and the sheep had put 8 fish inside the tank but now there are only 2!
Use a purple crayon to draw in the missing fish.

Pi For Kids Inc

SEQUENCES

Do you know how a shirt is made? Use a pencil ✏ to write the numbers 1, 2, 3 and 4 in the white squares below to tell the pictures should go.

LOGICAL THINKING

These little bears are looking at the big Ferris wheel. The Ferris wheel carts must be colored in the pattern red blue yellow . Color in the white carts with the right color to complete the pattern.

Pi For Kids Inc.

CRITICAL THINKING

Which one animal below will never appear in a zoo?
Use a red crayon to circle the animal below.

SEQUENCES

The pictures below tell a story about a little boy going to school but the pictures are not in the right order! use a pencil and write the numbers 1,2,3, or 4 in the white squares to tell the order that the pictures should go.

Pi For Kids Inc

SEQUENCES

The pictures below tell a story about five little birds growing up but the pictures are not in the right order! Use a pencil and writ th numbers 1, 2 ,3 , or 4 in the white squares below to tell the order that the pictures should go.

OBSERVATION

These two little bears are lost and need to get back to their mother. Use a green crayon to trace the right path to the mother bear.

SEQUENCES

The pictures below tell a story about how crops get harvested but the pictures are not in the right order! Use a pencil and write the numbers 1, 2, 3 or 4 in the white squares below to tell the order that the pictures should go.

FINDING DIFFERENCES

What is different about the pictures below? Use an orange crayon to circle 4 differences in the second picture.

Pi For Kids Inc

FINDING DIFFERENCES

What is different about the pictures below? Use a blue crayon to circle 4 differences in the second picture.

FINDING DIFFERENCES

What is different about the pictures below? Use a blue crayon to circle 4 differences in the second picture.

FINDING DIFFERENCES

What is different about the pictures below? Use a blue crayon to circle 4 differences in the second picture.

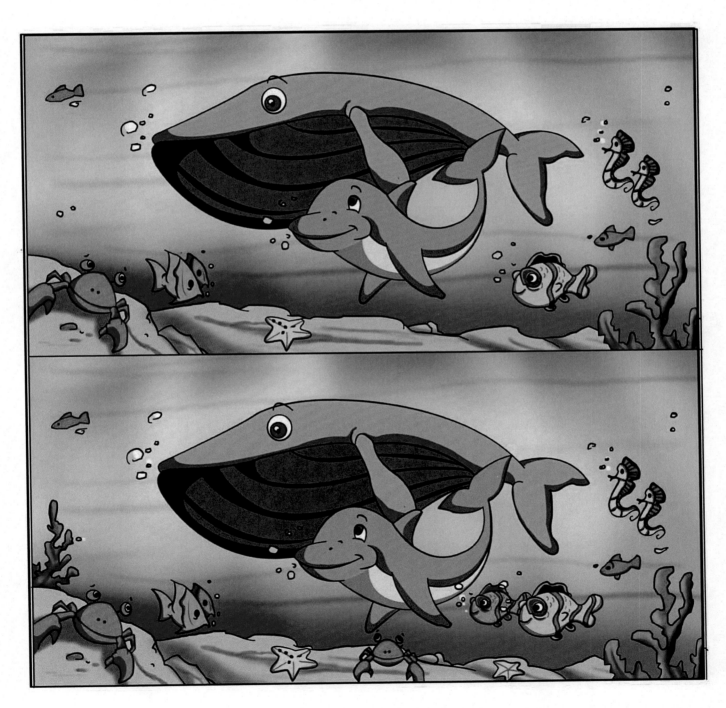

 # FINDING DIFFERENCES

What is different about the pictures below? Use an orange crayon to circle 4 differences in the second picture.

 # FINDING DIFFERENCES

What is different about the pictures below? Use a red crayon to circle 4 differences in the second picture.

Use a pencil ✏ to draw a line matching the top circles to what happens next on the lower pictures.

Pi For Kids Inc

LOGICAL THINKING

Use a pencil ✏ to draw a line matching the top circles to what happens next on the lower pictures.

OBSERVATION

The tigers are playing peek-a-boo in the woods. Find the tigers and use a pencil to write the number in the circle at the bottom of the page.

 # CRITICAL THINKING

The cat invited his best friends to dinner. Are you ready for dinner? Oops, one person doesn't have dinner yet.
Who is it? Why is this so?

 CRITICAL THINKING

Two little pigs are building houses. How many triangles did they use to build each roof? Use a pencil to write the number in the circle.

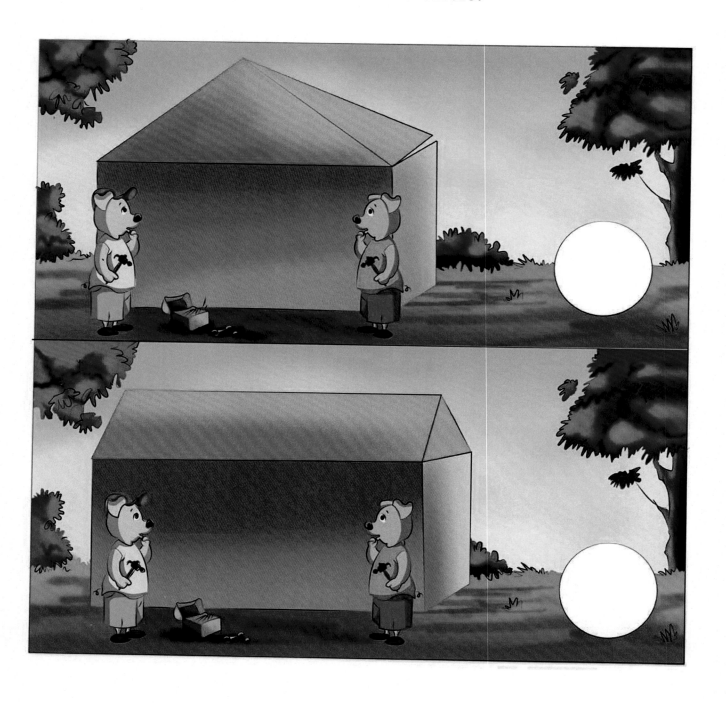

Pi For Kids Inc

 # CRITICAL THINKING

There are three different animals racing to see who can drink the smoothie the fastest. Use a blue crayon to circle the drink that will be drank the fastest.

VISUAL SKILLS

The elephant and the lion are in the park playing on the seesaw. Use a green crayon ✏ to circle which animal is heavier?

COUNTING

The kids are very happy because they have lollipops. Do you know how many lollipops do the children have? Use a pencil to write the correct number of lollipops in the circle.

COUNTING

Can you help the two frogs count how many fish are there in the lake? Use a pencil to write the correct number of fish in the circle.

OBSERVATION

The little girl likes to look at her beautiful clothing in the mirror. Do you know how many children are in the picture? Use a pencil ✏ to write the correct number of people in the circle.

Spring is here. The flowers are blooming! Do you know how many different kinds of animals are in the picture? Use a pencil to write the correct number of types of animals in the circle.

CORRELATION

The three monkeys are wondering how to match the pajamas. Can you help them? Use a green crayon to draw lines to match the pajamas.

DISTINGUISHING

Two bears are playing with their blocks on the floor. They need to pick all the blocks with a NUMBER on them. Use a red crayon to circle all the blocks with a NUMBER on them.

Pi For Kids Inc

OBSERVATION

A baby bear and its mother need to visit a friend but first they need to cross the lake. Use a red crayon to circle the object that the baby bear and its mother should take.

COLORING

The clown performed a magic trick and both rows of cups are exactly the same colors. Use crayons red 🖍 yellow 🖍 and blue 🖍 to color the second row of cups.

Pi For Kids Inc

ASSOCIATIONS

The monkeys have messed up the bedroom. Use a pencil to connect each pillow with the same colored bed.

 # LOGICAL THINKING

Today's weather has a very strong wind and it is blowing all the flowers and all of the girls' hair. Use a brown crayon to draw the direction of the wind.

Pi For Kids Inc

CRITICAL THINKING

Before going to school, the mother called her four children to eat breakfast. Only David drank all his orange juice and ate all his eggs, but he did not eat his sausages. Use a pencil to circle which set of breakfasts is David's.

OBSERVATION

The elephant is celebrating his birthday today! Count the number of candles on the cake. Do you know how old he is? Use a pencil ✏ to write the correct number in the white circle.

Pi For Kids Inc

The animals are having a party in the jungle! How many different types of animals are there? Use a pencil to write the correct number in the circle below.

DISTINGUISHING

This little girl is getting her hair cut at the salon for the first time! Do you know what is needed for a haircut? Use an orange crayon to circle the objects below.

COUNTING

Look at this beautiful underwater scene. How many sea horses do you see? Use a pencil to write the number of sea horses there are in the circle below.

OBSERVATION

This little pig is looking outside and the key hole shows what he sees. Use a blue crayon to circle the correct animal below that is standing outside the little pig's house.

Pi For Kids Inc

Brainstorm: IQ Training

OBSERVATION

The four pictures below each show some kind of movement. Each movement is either going up or going down. Use a yellow crayon ✏ to circle the one picture that shows a different movement than the other three.

DISTINGUISHING

Jessica is going to a birthday dinner and she has to dress formally. Which outfit should she wear? Use a red crayon to circle the correct outfit.

Pi For Kids Inc

OBSERVATION

The two girls below need to go to the bathroom. According to the sign, which way should they walk? Use a green crayon to circle the arrow on the sign that shows the way to the bathroom.

VISUAL SKILLS

There is a bag in the circle below and four people around it.
Who does the bag belong to?
Use a blue crayon to circle the correct person.

 # CRITICAL THINKING

There are a boy and girl ready to have a picnic together! Look at the four places and decide which place is the best for a picnic. Use an orange crayon to circle this place.

This boy just fell off his bicycle and scraped his knee! He needs to buy some bandages. Where should he go? Use a green crayon to circle the correct place.

CRITICAL THINKING

This mom and her daughter need to buy a birthday present. They want to buy a toy. Where should they go? Use a blue crayon to circle the correct place.

 # LANGUAGE ABILITY

Do you know the story of the tortoise and the hare? Ask your mom or dad to tell the story to you, then retell the story in your own words, using the pictures to help you if needed.

LANGUAGE ABILITY

Do you know the story of the boy who cried wolf? Ask your mom or dad to tell you the story and then retell the story to them using the pictures to help you.

OBSERVATION

The school bus below needs to get to school. Look at the road signs below. Which sign shows the way to school? Use a purple crayon ✏️ to draw the way how the school bus goes to school.

Pi For Kids Inc

SEQUENCES

This is a story about friends playing soccer game. The pictures are not in order. Use a pencil to write the numbers 1, 2, 3 or 4 in the white boxes to tell the order that they belong in.

LANGUAGE ABILITY

Do you know the story of Cinderella? Ask your mom or dad to tell the story to you, and then retell the story in your own words, using the pictures to help you if needed.

LANGUAGE ABILITY

Do you know the story of Snow White and the seven dwarfs? Ask your mom or dad to tell the story to you, and then retell the story in your own words, using the pictures to help you if needed.

Made in the USA
Middletown, DE
26 October 2015